Who Was Michael Jackson?

Who Was Michael Jackson?

By Megan Stine
Illustrated by Joseph J. M. Qiu

Grosset & Dunlap
An Imprint of Penguin Random House

For Matt—MS

To MJ, the greatest entertainer who ever lived,
and all his fans—JQ

GROSSET & DUNLAP
Penguin Young Readers Group
An Imprint of Penguin Random House LLC

Library of Congress Cataloging-in-Publication Data is available.

ISBN 978-0-448-48410-5 10 9 8 7 6 5 4 3 2 1

Contents

Who Was Michael Jackson?..1
Small House, Big Dreams..6
Sunny California..24
Big Changes..34
Fame and Fortune..47
Scarred and Burned..60
Buying the Beatles..65
Wacko Jacko..72
A Family of His Own..82
Too Little, Too Late..91
Timelines..102
Bibliography..104

Who Was Michael Jackson?

PASADENA, CALIFORNIA

Michael Jackson edged over to the side of the stage during a concert in 1983. He had purchased a spy hat, just like one in his latest music video. Michael had an idea for how to use the hat during the song he was going to sing—and he really hoped it would work.

The concert at the Pasadena Civic Auditorium was going to be broadcast on TV. Fifty million people would watch it. Many other famous singers had already performed. Now it was time for Michael's solo number.

Michael Jackson was already one of the biggest pop stars in the world. But he was never satisfied. He wanted to do something onstage no one would ever forget. He wanted the audience to go crazy!

As soon as the music started, Michael put on the hat and began to dance. Instantly, the audience jumped to its feet. They screamed and cheered. They recognized the hat and knew the song was "Billie Jean."

Wearing a sparkly black jacket, a silver shirt, and one white glove, Michael did dance moves that no one had ever seen before! He had practiced them in his kitchen the night before. His legs twitched. His hips jerked. His foot thumped. He threw the hat offstage in a smooth move that made the audience go wild again.

And then, in the middle of the song, he did something amazing. He slid backward, while making it look like he was walking forward. He called it the Moonwalk! The Moonwalk only lasted five seconds, but it was magical.

By the end of the song, everyone was standing.

The crowd was cheering. His whole family kissed him when he came offstage. No one would ever forget that Moonwalk. In fact, it became Michael Jackson's most famous move.

But was Michael happy? Not completely. He was thrilled that people loved the show. But he thought his dance could have been better. He hadn't stayed up on his toes long enough after the big spin at the end of the Moonwalk.

For Michael Jackson, nothing was ever good enough. He always wanted to be perfect. That's what made him work so hard to achieve his dreams—to become the best-selling singer of all time. That's what drove him to become the King of Pop.

Chapter 1
Small House, Big Dreams

Michael Joseph Jackson was born in Gary, Indiana, on August 29, 1958. The Jackson house was tiny and already crowded. Michael had four older brothers and two sisters. Maureen, called Rebbie, was the oldest. Next came Jackie, then Tito, Jermaine, LaToya, and Marlon. A few years after Michael was born, Randy came along. Janet Jackson was the baby of the family, born eight years after Michael.

Michael's mother, Katherine, worked part-time at a Sears department store. His father, Joseph, worked at a local steel mill. Joe Jackson earned only thirty dollars a day. To make extra money, he had a small band called the Falcons. They played in local bars and clubs around Indiana.

Joe played guitar, and the band practiced in the Jacksons' small house.

Both of Michael's parents had always loved music. His mother sang and played the clarinet and piano. Music was a big part of family life.

Joe Jackson was a very strict father. He had lots of rules. None of the kids were allowed to touch his guitar—ever! He kept it in a closet so they wouldn't be tempted to play it when he wasn't home.

One day, Tito, Jackie, and Jermaine sneaked into the closet and took the guitar to Tito's room.

Michael and his brothers watched as Tito figured out how to play chords. Tito had been studying their father carefully.

Little by little, Tito taught himself how to play. Katherine knew he was sneaking the guitar out, but she didn't tell her husband. She knew how mad he would be!

Then, one day, one of the strings on the guitar broke. Tito couldn't fix it, so he just put the guitar back in the closet and hoped his father wouldn't notice.

Of course Joe saw the broken string. All the boys were terrified, because their father could be so mean. Michael said that Joe hit the kids when they did something wrong. But this time Katherine spoke up. She told Joe that the boys were good singers—and that Tito could really play.

Joe handed Tito the guitar. "Let me see what you can do," he said.

As soon as Joe saw that his sons had talent, he wasn't angry. He brought home a shiny red guitar for Tito. Everyone in the family got music lessons, either at school or after school. Pretty soon, Jackie, Tito, Jermaine, Marlon, and Michael formed a band. They would become the Jackson 5.

At first Jermaine was the lead singer. Michael played the bongo drums. But it didn't take long for everyone to realize that Michael was the real star. He sang with so much feeling. When Michael entered a talent contest at school, his teachers cried at the sound of his beautiful voice.

As time went by, Joe Jackson decided to put everything into his sons' music careers. The family didn't have much money, but Joe spent all they had on musical instruments.

The Jackson boys had to rehearse every single day after school. There was no time to go outside or play. If anyone made a mistake while rehearsing, Joe punished them. Sometimes he hit them with his belt!

Michael didn't make many mistakes singing. But one time he was late for band practice. Sometimes he broke the rules around the house, too. Joe punished him for those things. When Joe hit Michael, sometimes Michael fought back. He would try to punch his father! Once, he threw a shoe at him! That made Joe madder still, and he beat Michael all the more.

Michael hated the way his father treated him, but he loved singing and dancing. He was happy when he was performing.

When the band was ready, Joe got them a job at a local nightclub called Mr. Lucky's. Michael was only six years old at the time!

By the time he was eight years old, he was working six nights a week. The Jackson 5 had to play five shows every night. Sometimes they played in bars or nightclubs.

Michael saw a lot of things he was too young to see. He got home late each night, too. He barely got enough sleep to go to school the next day.

Michael's mother worried about him. She was a very religious person. She had taken Michael to church and taught him never to swear. She didn't think he should be hanging out in bars.

But Joe was determined to make his sons a success. As the band got better, Joe started entering them in talent contests around town and even in distant cities. They always won. In Chicago, they won an important talent contest three weeks in a row.

Meanwhile, Joe decided it was time for the band to make a record. Their dream was to go to Motown. More than anything, Michael and his brothers wanted to record their music for the Motown label.

MOTOWN

MOTOWN WASN'T THE NAME OF A TOWN OR CITY—IT WAS THE NAME OF A FAMOUS RECORD LABEL IN DETROIT, MICHIGAN. IT WAS NAMED *MOTOWN* BECAUSE DETROIT'S NICKNAME WAS "THE MOTOR CITY," SINCE CARS WERE MADE THERE. THE MOTOWN SOUND COMBINED SOUL MUSIC AND POP MUSIC. MOTOWN GROUPS WERE ALMOST ALL AFRICAN AMERICAN—STEVIE WONDER, THE TEMPTATIONS, AND GLADYS KNIGHT AND THE PIPS. THEY WERE POPULAR WITH EVERYONE, THOUGH—BLACK AND WHITE LISTENERS ALIKE.

No matter how many times Joe tried, he couldn't get Motown to pay attention to the Jackson 5. Finally, Joe decided that Motown would have to notice them if they won the biggest talent contest of all time—at the Apollo Theater in New York City.

The Apollo is a famous theater in Harlem, an African American neighborhood.

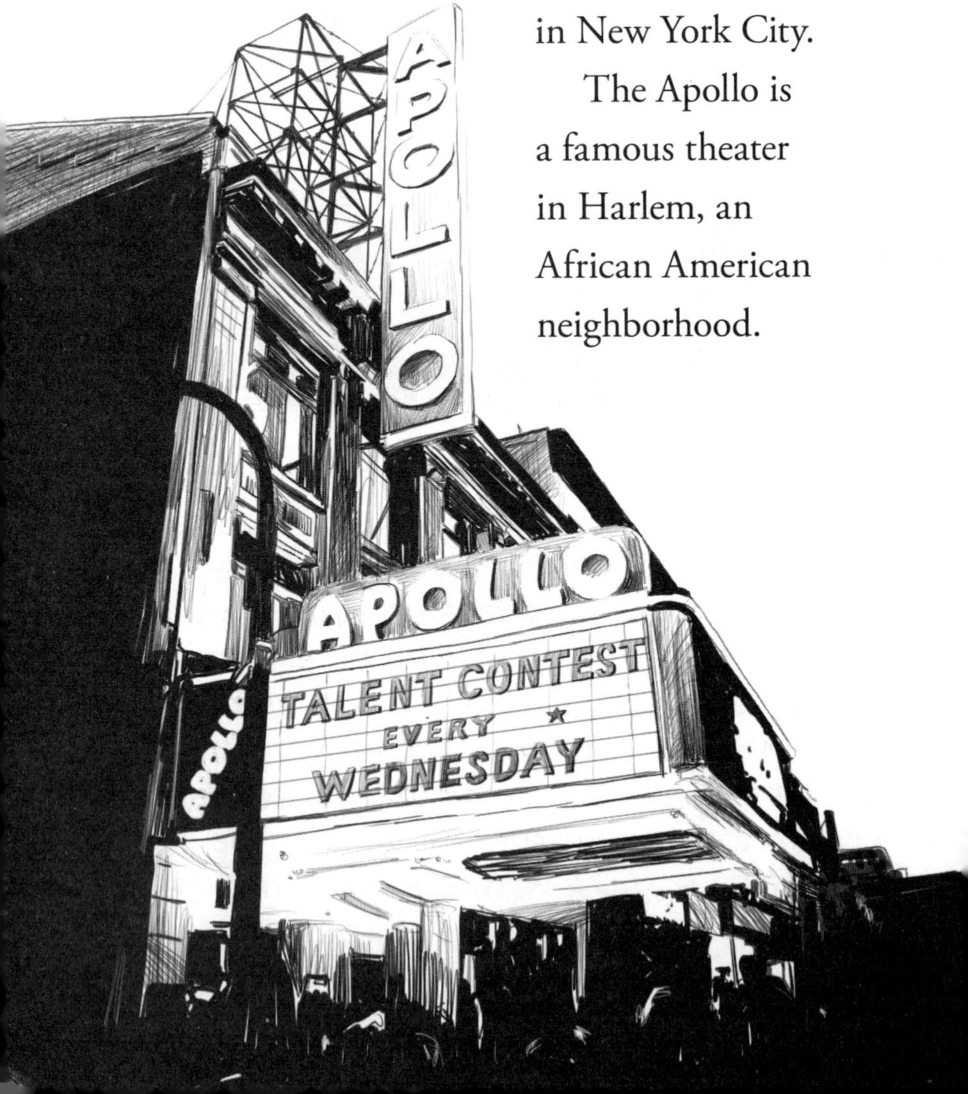

All the singers Michael loved had performed at the Apollo—people like James Brown and Stevie Wonder. A talent contest had been held there every Wednesday night for years.

So in the summer of 1967, when Michael was nine years old, Joe put all five of his boys into the family's VW bus and drove to New York City. Next stop, the Apollo!

Michael was dazzled by the huge, fancy theater. He even loved the microphone—it rose right up out of the floor. Part of a tree trunk was near the stage. It was supposed to be good luck to rub the tree before going onstage. So of course that's what Michael and his brothers did.

But the Jackson 5 had something better than luck—they had talent.

They won the talent show. Now would Motown call?

When they got home, Joe Jackson made a new rule. Phone calls could never last more than five minutes. Joe didn't want the line to be busy when Motown tried to reach them.

For months, they didn't hear from Motown. So Joe Jackson decided to accept an offer from a local record company called Steeltown. It was just a small studio in Gary, Indiana, but they recorded the first Jackson 5 song. It was called "Big Boy." Radio stations played it, and Joe sold lots of copies of it. But the Jackson 5 weren't going to get famous that way.

Finally, in July 1968, the call from Motown came. Michael and his brothers piled into their VW bus and drove to Detroit. They were going to sing for the head of the record company—Berry Gordy. If he liked them, they'd get a record deal!

BERRY GORDY

As soon as Berry Gordy heard the Jacksons sing, he knew what a superstar Michael could be. He told them, "I'm going to make you kids the biggest thing in the world." He promised that their first record would be number one on the music charts.

Michael Jackson was only ten years old—but he was on his way to becoming a legend.

Chapter 2
Sunny California

In 1969, Berry Gordy moved his Motown offices to Los Angeles, California—and the Jackson 5 moved with him. Gordy wanted them to live in California so they could record music there. Joe and Katherine Jackson were still back in Indiana. They were closing up their house so they could move to LA, too.

For a while, Michael lived part-time with Berry Gordy. The rest of the time, he lived down the street with a neighbor. The neighbor was a famous singer named Diana Ross!

Diana Ross was the star of a Motown group called the Supremes. She taught Michael about art and music. She took him to museums and taught him to draw.

DIANA ROSS

Michael loved Diana Ross. Living with her was one of the most special times in his life. He loved California, too. It was almost always sunny outside. He couldn't believe there were oranges on the trees. He and his brothers went to Disneyland.

Pretty soon, Berry Gordy brought the Jackson boys into his new recording studio. He had a song for them. It was called "I Want You Back."

Berry Gordy made the boys record it over and over again. For weeks! Michael listened to every word Berry Gordy said. Little by little, Michael was learning all about the music business—and he was learning from one of the best.

Berry Gordy turned the Jackson 5 into pop stars. He gave them new outfits and new hairstyles. He had someone teach the boys how to answer questions from reporters. They were tested on the answers! They were given lessons in table manners. Of course that was easy for Michael and his brothers. Their mother had insisted on good manners all their lives.

When “I Want You Back” came out in November 1969, it sold two million copies in six weeks! It was a number one hit, just as Berry Gordy had promised. Their next three singles were number one hits, too. The Jackson 5 were stars. And Michael Jackson was the most famous one in the group.

They did television shows with Diana Ross. They signed autographs. They went on the *Ed Sullivan Show*—a famous Sunday-night TV show. It was the same show where the Beatles had performed.

They played concerts in huge arenas like Madison Square Garden in New York. Mobs of fans—screaming girls—crowded around Michael wherever he went. Michael loved performing. He was never happier than when he was onstage. But he didn't like being crushed by fans. Sometimes girls scratched his face by accident. It was scary!

To avoid the crowds of fans, Michael and his brothers hid in their hotel rooms most of the time. They didn't have much freedom, but they did have a lot of fun together. They made fake phone calls. Then they giggled and hung up. They ordered room-service meals for other people's rooms. They held races in the hallways and had pillow fights. Michael loved to play pranks and practical jokes. His brothers did, too. Sometimes they dropped water balloons on people from the hotel windows!

Now the Jacksons were rich enough to buy their own fancy house in California. Joe and Katherine bought a house not far from Hollywood. The whole family lived there together for many years.

His early teen years were good times for Michael. He was still working nonstop, but at least he was having some fun in his time off.

But as Michael got older, he got hit with all the problems that teenagers face. Except he wasn't like other teenagers. He was a famous singer. It was a lot harder to grow up being Michael Jackson—rich, famous, and with everyone watching all the time.

Chapter 3
Big Changes

By the time Michael was fourteen years old, he was miserable about the way he looked. He wasn't a cute little kid anymore. Often fans were surprised or disappointed when they met him. Some didn't even recognize him! They were hoping to meet the person who was on the cover of the Jackson 5 albums. Now he was a skinny teenager, growing tall.

The growth spurt wasn't the worst part. The worst part was his face. It broke out in pimples. His father and brothers teased him about it all the time. They teased him about his nose, too, saying it was too big.

Michael couldn't stand to look in the mirror. He even washed his face in the dark, so he wouldn't have to look at himself!

From then on, Michael became super shy. He spoke in a very soft voice. He couldn't look people in the eye. He didn't even want to go out in public.

Michael's father didn't show much respect for Michael's feelings. Sometimes he brought fans into Michael's hotel room—while Michael was sleeping! Michael would wake up, and his fans would be right there, staring at him.

As time went on, Michael focused more and more on looking better. For Michael that meant finding ways to cover up his face.

Other things were changing in Michael's life, too. As he got older, he wanted to have more control over his own music. He wanted to write his own songs.

Michael talked to Berry Gordy about it, but Gordy said no.

So in 1976, the Jacksons left Motown. Michael was almost eighteen years old. Joe made a deal with CBS Records for $3.5 million. That was a huge amount of money. Best of all, now Michael could write his own songs and control how the records sounded.

The only problem was that Jermaine Jackson didn't want to leave Motown. He was an adult now—and he had married Berry Gordy's daughter. So Jermaine quit the band. Randy Jackson took Jermaine's place. From then on,

they couldn't call themselves the Jackson 5. Motown owned the name. So they just called themselves The Jacksons.

Michael was sorry to leave Berry Gordy, but Michael was a smart businessman by now.

A year later, Michael got an exciting call from Diana Ross. She wanted him to be in a movie with her. Diana was going to star in *The Wiz.* The story was based on *The Wizard of Oz*, but it was set in New York City. Michael would get to play the Scarecrow. He was so happy because he had to wear a lot of makeup. It covered up his pimples. He also loved dancing in the film.

Diana complained that Michael learned his dances too fast and it made everyone else look bad. Michael couldn't help it. When it came to dancing, he was just that good.

The Wiz was not a hit. In fact, it was a flop. But Michael had loved making the movie. That was part of his dream now—to become a movie star.

On the set of *The Wiz,* Michael became good friends with a man who would change his life in many ways. That man was Quincy Jones.

QUINCY JONES

FRED ASTAIRE (1899–1987)

FRED ASTAIRE WAS ONE OF THE MOVIE STARS MICHAEL JACKSON LOVED. ASTAIRE WAS ALSO THE MOST FAMOUS DANCER IN AMERICA. HE WAS A TAP DANCER WHO MOVED ALMOST LIKE A BALLET DANCER. HE MADE MANY MOVIES WITH FANTASTIC DANCES IN THEM. IN ONE MOVIE, FRED ASTAIRE DANCED RIGHT UP THE SIDE OF A WALL—AND THEN SEEMED TO DANCE ON THE CEILING!

MICHAEL STUDIED FRED ASTAIRE'S DANCE MOVES. WHEN HE WROTE A BOOK ABOUT HIS OWN LIFE, MICHAEL PUT A NOTE IN THE FRONT. IT SAID, "THIS BOOK IS DEDICATED TO FRED ASTAIRE."

THE DAY AFTER MICHAEL FIRST DID THE MOONWALK ON TV, HE GOT A PHONE CALL FROM FRED ASTAIRE. FRED WAS CALLING TO TELL MICHAEL HE COULD REALLY MOVE!

Quincy was a brilliant record producer, just like Berry Gordy. But Quincy didn't work for Motown. He worked for himself. Like Berry, he was kind and helpful to Michael. One day, on the movie set, Quincy heard Michael pronounce a word wrong. Very quietly, he told Michael how to say it the right way. Michael was so grateful. From that moment on, the two of them were friends. Quincy became like a father to Michael.

The timing was perfect for Michael. Now that Michael had left Motown, he was getting ready to make some changes in his own music. Quincy Jones was the right person to help make that happen.

In August 1979, Michael put out a solo album produced by Quincy. The album was called *Off the Wall*. Quincy talked other big stars into writing songs for the album. Paul McCartney—one of the Beatles—wrote one of the songs.

PAUL McCARTNEY

That same month, Michael turned twenty-one. Now he was old enough to make all his own decisions.

His first decision was a big one. He decided to fire his manager. But his manager was his father! Michael knew that his father had done a pretty good job for their family at first. He had created the Jackson 5 and brought them to Motown.

But Michael didn't want Joe running his life anymore. From now on, Michael was going to run his own life—and no one would be able to tell him what to do.

Chapter 4
Fame and Fortune

JOHN BRANCA

Now that Joe wasn't managing Michael's career, Michael needed to hire someone smart to help him. The first person he hired was a lawyer named John Branca. Over the next several years, Branca helped Michael get the best deals a record company had ever offered a singer up to that time.

Michael's first solo album with CBS was a big success. Four songs from the album were in the top ten on the music charts. In 1980, Michael won a Grammy Award—the highest award in the music business.

But was he happy?

No. Michael was upset because he only won *one* Grammy.

Michael was angry because the award was for

Best Male R&B Vocal Performance. "R&B" stands for "rhythm and blues." Most R&B singers are African American. Michael felt the Grammys were saying, "That's a great album—for a black singer. But it's not good enough for the rest of pop music."

Michael was determined to win Record of the Year next time.

With Quincy as the producer, Michael went into the studio in 1982 and started recording new songs. He recorded four he had written himself. One song was a duet. Paul McCartney sang it with him. It was called "The Girl Is Mine."

The album, called *Thriller*, also had other huge hits on it. "Billie Jean" and "Beat It"—both written by Michael—each went straight to number one on the charts. So did the song

"Thriller," which was written by someone else.

Before long, *Thriller* became the best-selling album of all time. It sold ten million copies the first year it came out, 1983. Over the years, it sold over one hundred million copies. No album has ever sold more copies than *Thriller*. In just four years, Michael earned more than $190 million.

What made *Thriller* such a huge success? Many things. First, Quincy and Michael worked so well together. They made musical magic happen.

Second, Michael was at the peak of his powers as an entertainer. He had been in the music business for nineteen years. He was a pro. He knew he needed to take his time—just as Berry Gordy had taught him—recording the songs over and over until they were perfect.

Sometimes Michael stayed up all night memorizing lyrics. Then the next day, they turned the lights out in the studio and recorded in the dark. That put Michael in a private mood, so he could put all his emotions and feelings into the song.

Michael and Quincy spent many months recording the album. They remixed the music over and over again, to get the sound just right.

Another reason *Thriller* was such a huge hit was because of its music videos. Michael thought of them as mini movies. He put all his energy and talent into them. The first one was for "Billie Jean."

At first, though, Michael couldn't get his videos on television.

Why not?

MTV, the new music-video channel, had only been around for one year. MTV thought their viewers only wanted to see white performers.

The president of CBS Records called up MTV. He gave them a warning. He said that MTV wouldn't be allowed to play music videos by famous white stars at CBS—like Bruce Springsteen and Billy Joel—unless they played Michael Jackson.

BRUCE SPRINGSTEEN

So MTV gave in. They played the "Billie Jean" video. That made all the difference. *Thriller* suddenly became a number one album on all the music charts—not just the "black music" charts!

Michael made two more incredible videos from *Thriller*. The first one was for the song "Beat It." It was a video about street gangs. Michael used real gang members from Los Angeles to act in it.

His best, biggest, and most expensive music video was for the song "Thriller" itself. Michael wanted it to look as if he were changing into a werewolf. He hired a director of horror movies. The video even had a dance scene with zombies.

When it was time for the Grammy Awards, Michael got twelve nominations for the *Thriller* album. He was so happy, he whooped and screamed and danced around the house.

On the night of the Grammy Awards, he won eight times! "Beat It" won Record of the Year. *Thriller* won Album of the Year.

Shortly after that, Michel was invited to the White House to meet President Ronald Reagan. Would this be enough to make Michael Jackson happy? Was he finally satisfied with his success?

DID MICHAEL HAVE PERFECT PITCH?

PERFECT PITCH IS THE ABILITY TO NAME ANY MUSICAL NOTE, JUST BY HEARING IT.

MICHAEL JACKSON HAD NOT BEEN TRAINED TO READ MUSIC, SO HE COULDN'T NAME THE NOTES. BUT HE WAS JUST AS IN TUNE AS SOMEONE WITH PERFECT PITCH. MICHAEL NEVER HIT A BAD NOTE—AND IT DROVE HIM CRAZY WHEN OTHER PEOPLE DID.

ONE TIME, MICK JAGGER FROM THE ROLLING STONES SANG WITH MICHAEL AND HIT A BAD NOTE. MICHAEL NEVER WANTED TO SING WITH HIM AGAIN. HE SAID MICK SANG FLAT!

QUINCY JONES'S RECORDING ENGINEER SAID THAT MICHAEL JACKSON WAS ONE OF THE FEW PEOPLE WHOSE SINGING NEVER HAD TO BE FIXED IN THE STUDIO. IT WAS ALWAYS PERFECT, JUST THE WAY HE SANG IT.

Chapter 5
Scarred and Burned

After *Thriller*, Michael Jackson was the most famous pop star in the world.

Still, there was a deep sadness in him. It was probably left over from his unhappy childhood. He felt lonely. It seemed as if no one could understand him.

To the outside world, Michael looked like the huge star he was. He wore fabulous clothes and costumes onstage. Fans everywhere tried to copy him. One of his most famous costumes was a military jacket. It was covered in gold braids, sparkly rhinestones, and jewels. His hair was long and wavy. He often wore sunglasses.

On the inside, though, he was still shy and didn't feel good about his looks. Michael had a

skin disorder and wore a lot of makeup to conceal it. He also used a skin-bleaching cream.

He had already had two nose jobs. Nose jobs are surgeries to make someone's nose smaller.

Then, in January 1984, Michael had a terrible accident. He was shooting an ad for Pepsi, in a big auditorium in LA. Crowds of fans were in the audience, watching. Michael was supposed to walk down some steps on the stage. Sparks and fireworks were going off beside him. All at once, his hair caught on fire!

At first, Michael didn't even realize what had happened. He kept dancing and spinning. Then his hands suddenly flew up to his head.

Michael was rushed to the hospital. He had very bad burns. He had to have surgery. His scalp would never really be the same. Afterward, the doctors gave him drugs for the pain.

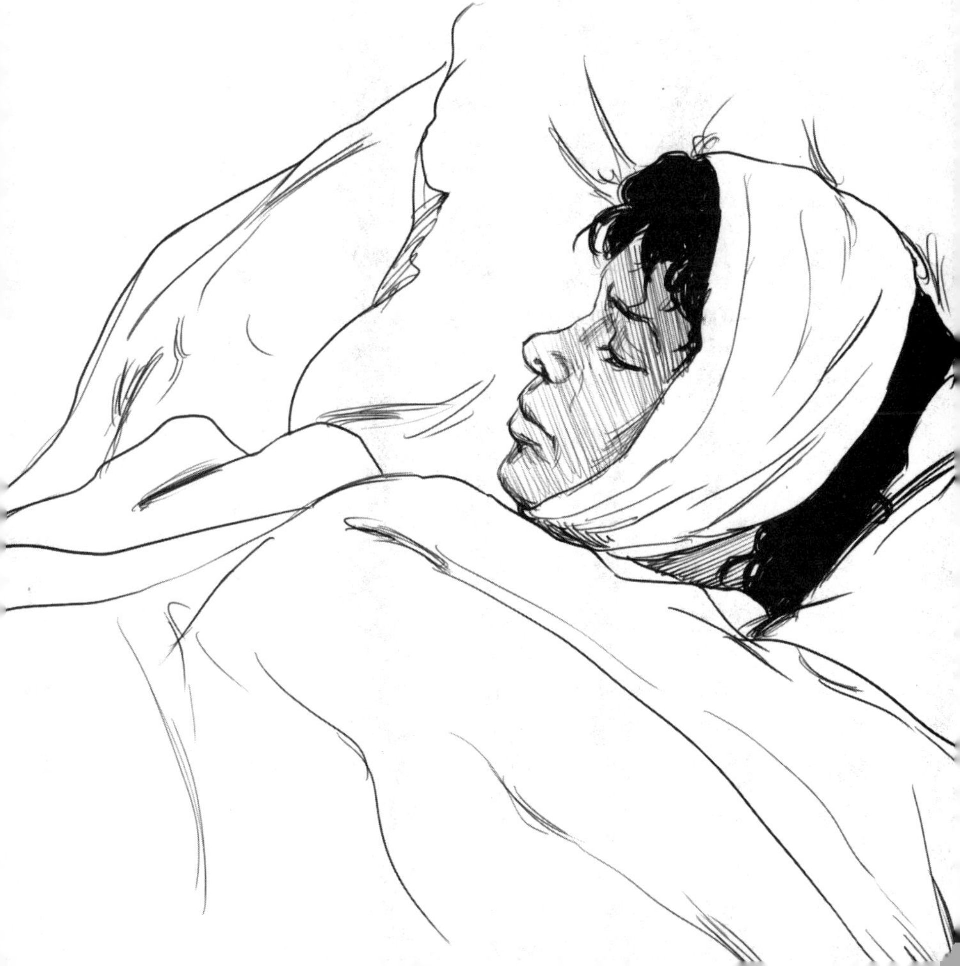

Up till then, Michael Jackson had never used drugs. But he took the pain pills that his doctors gave him. Over time, he got addicted to those drugs and didn't want to stop.

Two good things came out of the Pepsi accident, though. Pepsi gave Michael $1.5 million to donate to the burn center at the hospital where he had been treated.

Pepsi also gave Michael a deal of just over $5.2 million to make more Pepsi ads. John Branca helped Michael make the deal. Michael was already famous and loved by millions. But now he was about to become one of the richest men in the music world.

Chapter 6
Buying the Beatles

Michael had been in the music business long enough to know how it worked. Often, the record companies got rich, while the singers and songwriters didn't. Why? A big part of the money came from owning the rights to the songs. Sure, the singers got paid for each record that they sold. But sometimes, they only got one penny per copy—or less! They couldn't get rich that way.

The Jackson 5 had never owned the rights to their own songs. For one thing, they hadn't written them. Besides, Berry Gordy made all his singers sign a contract saying that Motown owned the songs.

The Beatles had the same thing happen to them. They wrote so many great songs—but they had given away the rights. The Beatles made a lot of money from their records and ticket sales to their concerts. They made money from movies and TV. Still, they didn't own their own songs—and that's where the big money was.

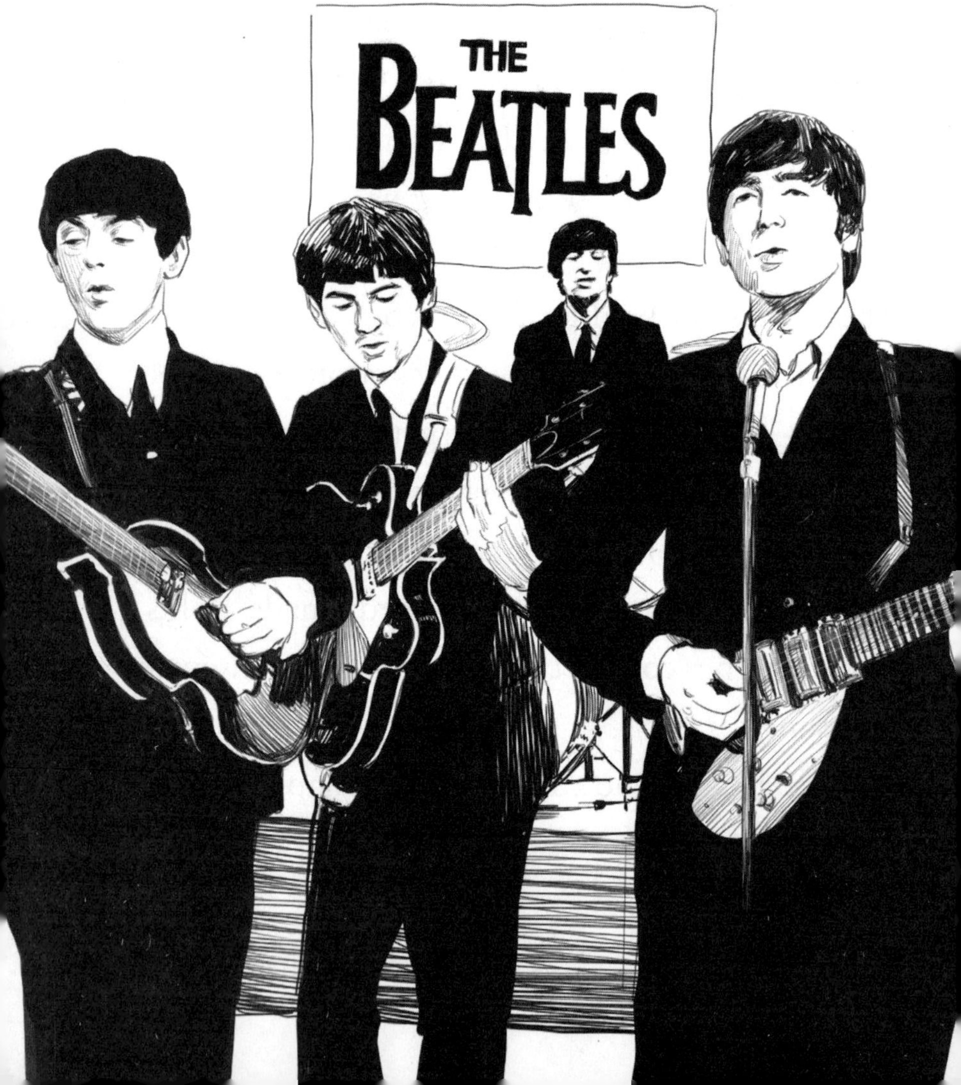

When Michael met Paul McCartney in 1981, Paul told him a secret. He was buying up the rights to other singers' big hits. Paul had a list of songs he had bought. He called it his catalog. He was getting rich from owning other people's music. Paul said Michael should do the same thing. So Michael asked his lawyer, John Branca, to keep an eye out for songs that Michael could buy.

One day in 1984, Branca said a new catalog of songs was for sale—the Beatles' songs! Michael couldn't believe it. He wanted that catalog, no matter how much he had to pay for it.

It was going to be tricky, though. What if Paul McCartney wanted to buy his own songs back?

John Branca asked Paul McCartney's lawyer whether Paul was planning to do that. The lawyer said no—it was too expensive. But Paul didn't realize that Michael Jackson wanted to buy the Beatles' songs. If he had known, he might have changed his mind.

Branca offered $30 million for the catalog. Other people bid higher. The price kept going up. Pretty soon, some of the smartest people in New York and Hollywood were telling Michael he was crazy. He was spending way too much money.

Michael didn't listen. It took a couple of months, but Branca finally won the bidding war. Michael Jackson bought the Beatles' songs for $47.5 million.

Buying the Beatles' songs turned out to be the smartest thing Michael ever did. Within ten years, the catalog was worth more than $150 million. It brought in payments of $10 million to Michael each year. Today, it's worth $1 billion!

Paul McCartney *was* upset about it, though. He called Michael to talk. After all, they were friends.

Paul said that just like Michael and the Jackson 5, the Beatles had gotten a very bad deal when they were young. Now that Michael owned the songs, would he consider giving the Beatles a better share of the profits?

Michael said no. Even though Michael had a soft voice and shy personality, he was a hard businessman. And to him, this was just a business deal.

"WE ARE THE WORLD"

IN 1985, MICHAEL WROTE A SONG WITH LIONEL RICHIE CALLED "WE ARE THE WORLD." THE SONG WAS WRITTEN FOR CHARITY. MOST OF THE MONEY FROM THE RECORD SALES WOULD BE USED TO HELP STARVING PEOPLE IN THE AFRICAN COUNTRIES OF ETHIOPIA AND SUDAN.

QUINCY JONES PRODUCED THE RECORD. HE GOT A GROUP OF FAMOUS SINGERS TO COME INTO THE STUDIO ALL AT ONCE. BOB DYLAN WAS THERE. SO WERE BRUCE SPRINGSTEEN,

STEVIE WONDER, TINA TURNER, BILLY JOEL, CYNDI LAUPER, RAY CHARLES, DIANA ROSS, AND MANY MORE. OF COURSE MICHAEL JACKSON AND LIONEL RICHIE SANG SOLOS, TOO.

THE RECORD SOLD MILLIONS OF COPIES AND WON THREE GRAMMY AWARDS. A VIDEO OF THE RECORDING SESSION WAS SHOWN ON MTV. IT BECAME A HUGE HIT AS WELL. MORE THAN $63 MILLION WERE RAISED TO BUY FOOD, CLOTHING, AND MEDICINE.

Chapter 7
Wacko Jacko

Now that he was so rich, Michael could do almost anything he wanted. No one dared to tell him no—at least not his family or friends. Sometimes Branca did warn Michael not to do things. But even then, Michael just went ahead and followed his own heart.

A lot of the things Michael wanted to do seemed totally crazy.

In 1986, Michael visited a hospital and saw a glass box—like a clear coffin. It was called a hyperbaric chamber. It was for sick people who needed extra oxygen. Michael got inside the box and had his picture taken. Then he had the picture sent to newspapers. He said he slept in there every night, so he could live to be 150 years old.

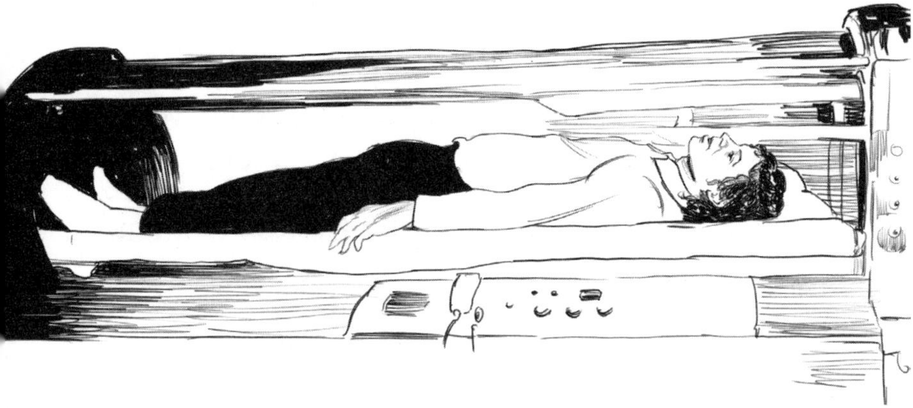

The story wasn't true. Michael was just kidding around. He had read a book by P. T. Barnum, a famous circus owner. Barnum wrote that there was no such thing as bad publicity. Michael thought that was true.

P. T. BARNUM

Next, Michael created another weird story. He let people think that he wanted to buy the Elephant Man's bones. The Elephant Man, Joseph Merrick, was a real person who lived in England in the 1800s. He was part of a circus sideshow. The circus put him on display because his face and hands were very deformed.

When the newspapers heard about this, they thought Michael Jackson had lost his mind. One newspaper called him "Wacko Jacko." The nickname stuck.

In 1988, Michael got a pet chimp named Bubbles. He told people he slept with the chimp. He took Bubbles to dinner with him.

Michael was rich and famous. Yet he seemed no happier than when he was younger. He still hated his looks. He kept having surgery on his face. Finally, he had so many that the tip of his nose was almost gone!

Michael had surgery to put a dimple in his chin. He started wearing a surgical mask over his face afterward to cover the scars until his chin healed. But some people thought Michael was just crazy and afraid of germs.

Michael looked very strange in some pictures. Newspapers kept calling him Wacko Jacko. It hurt his feelings. But he had tried to get attention in the wrong way. Now he regretted it—and wanted to get as far away from the public as he could.

In 1988, he found a good place to hide. He bought Neverland Valley Ranch in Santa Barbara County, California. It was nearly three thousand acres—much larger than most big city parks.

Neverland was like a dream come true for Michael. It was his private amusement park! It had a Ferris wheel, a small train, bumper cars, a pirate-ship ride, a roller coaster, a petting zoo, and much more. There were statues of children everywhere. Wild animals roamed around. A huge outdoor clock, as big as a building, was surrounded by the word *Neverland* spelled out in flowers. Of course there was a swimming pool, a movie theater, and a giant collection of video games. Michael also built a huge house for himself, and smaller guesthouses.

Michael had never had a real childhood—he had worked since he was five years old. At Neverland, he could play all day. It was perfect—except for one thing. Who could he enjoy it with?

Michael still loved his family, but he didn't want to live with them anymore. He felt his family asked him for things too often. They wanted him to tour with the The Jacksons again. Michael didn't want to do that.

So Michael moved into Neverland all by himself. It was a very private place, with a huge gate around it. Most of the time, Michael Jackson was very much alone.

TROUBLE

MICHAEL HAD ALWAYS LOVED SPENDING TIME WITH CHILDREN. WHENEVER HE COULD, HE FOUND WAYS TO BE KIND AND GENEROUS TO THEM. SOMETIMES HE VISITED SICK CHILDREN IN THE HOSPITAL. THEN HE'D INVITE THEM AND THEIR FAMILIES TO COME STAY AT NEVERLAND. HE BOUGHT BAGS OF TOYS AND SPENT HOURS PUTTING BATTERIES IN THEM. HE GAVE THE TOYS TO KIDS WHO CAME TO SEE HIM BACKSTAGE AT HIS CONCERTS.

AS TIME WENT BY, MICHAEL BECAME CLOSE FRIENDS WITH SEVERAL YOUNG BOYS. SOME PEOPLE THOUGHT HE WAS TOO CLOSE TO SOME OF THEM. SOMETIMES MICHAEL TOOK THE BOYS ON TOUR WITH HIM.

OVER TIME, ONE BOY'S PARENTS GREW WORRIED. THE BOY SAID MICHAEL HAD TOUCHED HIM IN A WAY GROWN-UPS SHOULD NOT TOUCH CHILDREN. IN 1993 THE POLICE GOT INVOLVED, AND STORIES CAME OUT IN THE NEWSPAPERS. MICHAEL DENIED EVERYTHING. HE SAID THAT THE PARENTS JUST WANTED MONEY FROM HIM AND WERE LYING TO GET IT. IN THE END, MICHAEL PAID THE FAMILY MILLIONS OF DOLLARS SO THAT THEY WOULD DROP THEIR CASE AGAINST HIM.

YEARS LATER, ANOTHER BOY SAID MICHAEL TOUCHED HIM IN A WAY THAT WAS WRONG. THIS TIME, MICHAEL HAD TO GO TO COURT. BUT MANY OF MICHAEL'S YOUNG FRIENDS WERE ON HIS SIDE. THEY CAME TO COURT TO SPEAK UP FOR HIM. THEY SAID MICHAEL HAD NEVER DONE ANYTHING WRONG TO THEM. AT THE END OF THE TRIAL, HE WAS FOUND NOT GUILTY AND DIDN'T GO TO JAIL. FOR THE REST OF HIS LIFE, MICHAEL INSISTED THAT HE HAD NEVER DONE ANYTHING WRONG.

Chapter 8
A Family of His Own

Michael had never dated much. For a short time, he went out with Tatum O'Neal. She had been a child actress and was the daughter of a movie actor. Michael liked Tatum because she understood what it was like to be a child in show business.

TATUM O'NEAL

A few years later, Michael went on dates with Brooke Shields. She too had been famous both as a child model and an actress. After that, he didn't have a girlfriend.

BROOKE SHIELDS

But when troubles came up in his life, he wanted someone who could help him and understand him. He was terribly lonely. He had lost touch with Diana Ross. He was taking drugs—prescription drugs, but he was taking too many of them. He needed help.

LISA MARIE PRESLEY

Michael called his friend Lisa Marie Presley. She was the daughter of Elvis Presley, the first rock superstar. Michael and Lisa Marie had been friends for years. Now they talked on the phone a lot while he was out of the country on tour. One day, on the phone, Michael asked Lisa if she would marry him. Lisa was married to someone else at the time. But she said yes. She would marry him after she got a divorce.

On May 26, 1994, Michael and Lisa Marie had a very secret wedding. It was in the Dominican Republic in the Caribbean. Michael didn't even tell his mother about the wedding. Lisa didn't tell her family, either.

THE KING AND THE KING OF POP

ELVIS PRESLEY WAS THE FIRST ROCK 'N' ROLL SUPERSTAR. LIKE MICHAEL JACKSON, HE BECAME FAMOUS FOR THE WAY HE MOVED ONSTAGE. HE ALSO MADE MOVIES AND WORE FLASHY COSTUMES IN HIS ACT. IN THE 1950S, TEENAGE GIRLS LOVED HIM, AND GUYS WANTED TO BE LIKE HIM. HE WAS SO FAMOUS, HE BECAME KNOWN AS "THE KING."

MICHAEL JACKSON WANTED A NICKNAME LIKE "THE KING." HE WANTED TO BE AS FAMOUS AS ELVIS HAD BEEN. IN 1988, MTV ASKED MICHAEL TO APPEAR ON THEIR MUSIC-VIDEO AWARDS SHOW. HE AGREED, BUT ONLY ON ONE CONDITION. FROM THEN ON, MTV HAD TO CALL HIM THE "KING OF POP" EVERY TIME THEY MENTIONED HIS NAME. IT WORKED—FROM THEN ON, EVERYONE CALLED HIM BY THAT ROYAL NICKNAME.

When they came back to America, Lisa and Michael kept the wedding secret for months. Michael knew that when the secret got out, there would be lots of publicity—and he was right.

The marriage lasted less than two years. One possible reason it ended was that Michael wanted to have children. But Lisa already had children. They divorced in 1996. But they stayed friends for a long time after that.

Michael remained determined to have children. If Lisa wouldn't have his baby, Michael would find someone else who would. The person he chose was another friend, a nurse named Debbie Rowe. Michael had met her at his skin doctor's office. Michael and Debbie talked on the phone all the time.

DEBBIE ROWE

When Debbie agreed to have Michael's baby and give it to him, he was thrilled.

He gave her lots of money and bought her a million-dollar house. He was very grateful that she was willing to have children with him without being his wife.

Michael's mother had a different idea, though. When Katherine found out that Debbie was pregnant, she wanted Michael to marry Debbie. Michael had always loved and respected his mother. He knew she was very religious. He couldn't say no to her about this.

So on November 13, Michael and Debbie got married in a hotel in Australia. Only about fifteen friends were there with them. Debbie and Michael both wore black.

On February 13, 1997, Debbie had a baby boy. Michael named him Prince Michael Jackson.

People thought the name was too fancy. Did Michael think his son was royalty? No. The truth was that Michael's own grandfather and great-grandfather were both named Prince. It was a family name.

Michael took the baby home to Neverland alone—without Debbie. A staff of nannies and nurses took care of the baby. Debbie never lived with Michael. She didn't act like the baby's mother.

Then on April 3, 1998, Debbie had another baby with Michael. This one was a girl. They named her Paris. The baby's full name was Paris Katherine Michael Jackson.

Again, Michael raised the baby without Debbie. She only saw the children a few times. Finally, Debbie decided she didn't want to be married to Michael any longer. She and Michael divorced in 1999.

A few years later, Michael announced to the world that he had a third baby. This time, Debbie wasn't the mother. Michael wouldn't say who the mother was. The baby boy was born on February 21, 2002. Michael named him Prince Michael II. His nickname was "Blanket." After that, Michael's older son was known as Prince Michael I.

Now Michael had a family, just as he had wanted. Would his life be easier? Were happier times ahead?

Sadly, the answer was no.

Chapter 9
Too Little, Too Late

All through the late 1980s and early 1990s, Michael continued to record exciting music. His album *Bad* came out in 1987. It sold millions and millions of copies. One song on the album was called "Man in the Mirror." It became one of Michael's favorite songs, even though he hadn't written it. The song talked about trying to change the world by changing yourself first. Michael donated all the money he earned from that song to a camp for children with cancer.

Michael's next album, released four years later, was titled *Dangerous.* It included one of his most interesting songs—a song called "Black or White." The words said that it didn't matter whether people were black or white. The music video showed dozens of faces—people of all colors—morphing or blending into one another. Almost every top-forty radio station in America played the song the first day it came out.

Michael was still a huge star and a brilliant, creative performer. But his personal life remained troubled. He started using prescription drugs again.

By 2005, he hadn't recorded a big hit album in years. He hadn't gone on tour. Some of his managers thought he was afraid his show wouldn't be good enough. If his show wasn't fabulous, Michael thought he'd be disappointing his fans.

For several years, Michael and his children lived in countries overseas. They lived in Bahrain in the Middle East for a long time. Then they moved to Ireland. Finally they moved back to the United States, to Las Vegas, Nevada. The whole time, Michael kept spending like a superstar. Every year, he spent twice as much money as he earned!

MICHAEL JACKSON'S LAS VEGAS HOUSE

By 2007, Michael was in terrible money trouble. He had borrowed a lot so that he could keep up his expensive lifestyle. But he had to pay his debts soon, and that might mean losing everything—including the Beatles' songs and Neverland.

Michael had to start working again. He needed to do big concerts and record a big album. So he agreed to do a concert series called "This Is It." Fifty concerts would be held in London, starting in 2009.

In the weeks leading up to the first concert, Michael rehearsed nonstop. Sometimes he felt good and enjoyed it. He was still a great singer and dancer. The backup singers would often watch and applaud. But Michael was worried sick.

He still wanted to be perfect. What if he couldn't deliver great shows for his fans? He couldn't sleep at night from all the worry.

DR. CONRAD MURRAY

Once again, he turned to drugs. To help him sleep, Michael hired a doctor named Conrad Murray. Doctors are only supposed to do what is good for a patient. But Dr. Murray did not do that. He injected Michael with the kind of drugs that are used in hospitals for people having surgery. The drugs were very dangerous. They knocked Michael out for the night. That was what Michael wanted.

On June 25, 2009, Michael Jackson died from an overdose of those drugs. Dr. Murray was charged with killing him accidentally. For his crime, he went to jail for two years.

When the world heard that Michael Jackson had died, millions of fans everywhere were shocked and sad. A huge memorial service was held in Los Angeles. It was broadcast on TV. At the funeral, many famous people spoke, including Berry Gordy. Diana Ross sent a message to be read aloud. Michael's daughter, Paris, spoke, too. She talked about how much she loved her father and missed him. Superstar singers performed songs in memory of Michael. Each of Michael's brothers wore a single white glove with sequins on it, to honor their brother. They sat in the front row with the rest of the family, including Michael's parents.

As part of the service, Jermaine Jackson sang Michael's favorite song, "Smile." The lyrics probably said a lot about how Michael Jackson felt much of the time. They said: "Smile, though your heart is aching. Smile, even though it's breaking."

Now that Michael was gone, people wanted to remember the good things about Michael. His talent was so huge. It had been a gift to millions all over the world. His singing and dancing had brought so much happiness to others.

Sadly, though, performing seems to have been the only way he found any happiness himself.

He was only fifty years old when he died, but he was already a legend. In fact, at the funeral, Berry Gordy said that "King of Pop" wasn't a big enough title for Michael. He said Michael Jackson had simply been the greatest entertainer who ever lived.

THE JACKSONS—
WHERE ARE THEY NOW?

AFTER MICHAEL'S DEATH, THE JACKSONS PERFORMED CONCERTS IN TRIBUTE TO MICHAEL ALL OVER THE WORLD.

JERMAINE JACKSON HAD A VERY SUCCESSFUL RECORDING CAREER OF HIS OWN. HE MADE SOLO ALBUMS AND WON A GRAMMY IN 1980. HE ALSO RECORDED DUETS WITH THE FAMOUS SINGER WHITNEY HOUSTON.

JACKIE, TITO, AND RANDY HAVE ALL PERFORMED OVER THE YEARS AS MUSICIANS ON OTHER PEOPLE'S ALBUMS.

MICHAEL'S YOUNGER SISTERS BOTH HAD CAREERS OF THEIR OWN. LATOYA RECORDED ALBUMS AND APPEARED ON REALITY TV SHOWS.

JANET JACKSON IS A HUGE STAR IN HER OWN RIGHT. SHE'S SOLD MILLIONS OF ALBUMS, PERFORMED AT THE SUPER BOWL, AND APPEARED ON TV AND IN MOVIES.

TIMELINE OF MICHAEL JACKSON'S LIFE

1958	Michael Jackson is born in Gary, Indiana
1967	Jackson 5 play the Apollo Theater in Harlem and win talent contest First record deal with Steeltown Records
1968	Jackson 5 sign a record deal with Motown Records
1969	Michael and family move to California
1970	Jackson 5 have three hit singles in one year
1976	Jackson 5 leave Motown Records and sign a deal with CBS
1978	Stars in *The Wiz* with Diana Ross
1979	Solo album *Off the Wall* produced by Quincy Jones
1983	Performs the Moonwalk on *Motown 25* television special *Thriller* is released and becomes best-selling album of all time
1984	Wins eight Grammy Awards Burned during filming of Pepsi commercial Buys the Beatles' songs
1985	Writes and records "We Are the World"
1988	Buys Neverland Ranch
1994	Marries Lisa Marie Presley
1996	Divorces Lisa Marie Presley and marries Debbie Rowe
1997	First son born, named Prince Michael Jackson
1998	Daughter born, named Paris Katherine Michael Jackson
2002	Second son born, named Prince Michael II
2005	Goes on trial and found not guilty
2009	Dies at age fifty

TIMELINE OF THE WORLD

West Side Story premieres in New York	1957
John Glenn becomes the first American to orbit Earth	1962
Martin Luther King Jr. gives his "I Have a Dream" speech President John F. Kennedy is assassinated	1963
Nelson Mandela is sentenced to life in prison in South Africa The Beatles appear on *The Ed Sullivan Show* for the first time	1964
Thurgood Marshall becomes the first black Supreme Court justice	1967
Martin Luther King Jr. is assassinated	1968
The Beatles announce that the band will be breaking up	1970
The Twenty-Sixth Amendment to the US Constitution lowers the voting age to eighteen	1971
Richard Nixon becomes the first US president to resign	1974
Elvis Presley dies	1977
Margaret Thatcher is the first woman to become prime minister of the United Kingdom	1979
MTV debuts	1981
The first albums on compact discs (CDs) are released	1982
The *Oprah Winfrey Show* airs on national television	1986
The Berlin Wall, separating East and West Berlin, is torn down	1989
Nelson Mandela becomes president of South Africa	1994
Apple launches the iPod	2001
Barack Obama becomes the president of the United States	2009

BIBLIOGRAPHY

Greenburg, Zack O'Malley. **Michael Jackson, Inc.: The Rise, Fall, and Rebirth of a Billion-Dollar Empire.** New York: Atria Books, 2014.

Jackson, Michael. **Moonwalk.** New York: Doubleday, 1988.

Taraborrelli, J. Randy. **Michael Jackson: The Magic, The Madness, the Whole Story, 1958–2009.** New York: Grand Central Publishing, 2009.

Whitfield, Bill, and Javon Beard, with Tanner Colby. **Remember the Time: Protecting Michael Jackson in His Final Days.** New York: Weinstein Books, 2014.